The Life of Little Lamb

Penelope Swart

Presentation by *BookLeaf Publishing*

Web: www.bookleafpub.com

E-mail: info@bookleafpub.com

ISBN: 9789357212595

First edition 2023

*For Socs, whose lessons will forever remain in
my heart forever.*

ACKNOWLEDGEMENT

I would like to acknowledge my tender and helpful parents and teachers that coached me through these poems, and my caring friends who inspired me. However, I would also like to recognise how much sheep are overlooked. People see them as the stupid flock animals. That is the stereotype that has grown over them. But I believe that is wrong. Sheep are intelligent, compassionate and curious. All it takes is to look past food and flock and to see in to their souls. Most farm animals are overlooked, if we took the time to understand them, entire universes of life and civilisation will be uncovered.

PREFACE

On the 23rd of August 2022, my life changed forever, we adopted an orphaned lamb. He came to us about to die, but we nurtured him back to health. He grew stronger and stronger, we knew that he would live. But as he kept extending and changing, we knew that a backyard is not the right place for a growing sheep. So we sent him back to the farm where he was born. It hurt to loose him, I didn't realise how much he helped me grow and how many values he taught me.

He thrived on the farm, he was growing stronger, he was eating well, he was making friends. But just after a week, he died. It hurt my heart like nothing I had ever experienced. So I decided to write about them, and uncover the unseen blossoms that are sheep.

Fate

At the end of fate,
Lays a bigger beginning,
With a misfit trait.

Spring Lamb

At the opening of Spring's eye,
His heart faced death with certainty.
He would not fall, he would not surrender,
Born, as life rose from slumber.

He seemed so full of soul and love,
His stride a secret promise.
He led us into clarity,
And cheered us on with hope.
He inspired so many hearts,
And annulled so many lies.

He felt like eternity,
A wall that could not be broke.
But at the setting of the sun,
As the fire burns dim,
He must move on.

The Dawn

The dawn will come,
Her fingers will touch the land,
Her light will colour the hills,
And all will be found,
But all is to be lost.
Our tread dies unheard,
Our world alight with sorrow,
We're a lock without a key,
A song without a tune.

That dawn has come,
The answer is near,
It's fleece is white as a snowy cloud,
And eyes as deep as seas.
But this dawn has no end,
And no beginning,
There is no clear path,
Just a tangle of trees,
And thoughts,
And hopes.
But it pulls me in,
And I find my key,
But it is to be taken again.

Life

Spring's steps were fragile,
They were gentle and warm,
They were hopeful.
They smelled of integrity,
And blinded us with light,
But an imposter came with Spring.
He was shakily breathing,
A ruined, broken lump.
He was small and hurt,
And lingered on death's doorstep,
But he would not die.

Death was now coming,
They were a bat,
They were a spider,
They were a snake.
Their seathe tasted of blood,
And their eyes were deep as the night.
Their shadow was growing darker,
And bones a dealthy white.
Their heart beat a cruel rhythm,
But no matter how hard they tried,
Socs would survive.

The Days

5

They were perfect days,
Bright, bouncing, joyful, shining,
But then, they were gone.

He Will Rise

Born from the ashes,
Fell from the sky,
Sank into dirt,
He will rise.

From the dark,
Before the dawn,
Hope dies unheard,
Everything we've waited for.
We start to doubt,
But we see him there,
We know in our hearts,
He will rise.

The clock kept ticking,
Turning softly,
As the years go by,
Meaning is lost.
We fall again,
But he will rise.

Beanstalk

He will grow.
Unseen and unheard he will sprout.
From what used to be a puppet of death,
Was the representative of life.
His spring grew ever stronger,
His bleat a bright, sweet song.
His connection to love grew deeper.
He forgave all our wrongs,
His beanstalk grew even thicker,
His leaves large and tough,
But in his core, in his heart,
It wasn't enough.

While his roots spread out further,
Under earth and stone,
And his tips grew above the clouds,
And turned a higher hue,
He smelled of sadness and sorrow,
A part of him not found.
While his beanstalk was still thriving,
He was all alone.
Yes, he had his human carers,
Who reached into his soul,
But unseen from all the people,
He sang an unheard song.

Safe and warm his beanstalk thrived,
But adventure called his roots,
While he lived,
He was not alive.

Gambolling Lamb

Springing through the fields,
Dancing through the daisies,
He was finally home.
Leaping, laughing, calling, found.
His step was young,
His heart beat strong,
His spirit would live forever long.

He frolloked in the paddocks, bright,
Flying into the gentle wind,
Like a bird he leapt.
A cloud giften legs,
And heart,
And soul.
Skipping through grassy hills,
His spirit flew into the sky,
Dancing in the sunshine,
Warm, and bright.
Not a care touched him there,
No cold lump of worry.
Just him and life and fun and love,
Skimming through the hills.

Flowers of all hues and shapes,
Painted nature's mound,

An artwork they drew,
A story bright but grim.
The trees spoke anceint songs,
Their roots carrying the stories.
The energy bounced into his willing hoves,
And helped him fly beyond.

While spining through bright hues of joy,
The breeze full of sweet, merry love
He was happy and full and complete,
His hunger was finally ceased,
And he could live forever.
But when the sun sank low,
And the winds from the south,
Carried stars across the sky,
He gazed up at the moon,
His playful gambol stopped,
He felt hungry again.

Daisy

Emotions trapped in objects,
Hues of rainbow, shining,
Dew drops collecting,
Dripping down to stories.
Flowers, gentle and lovely,
Have so much to tell,
Their stories confined,
But sought in farewell.

Ignored and shoved aside,
Hidden behind the normal,
The smaller flowers bloom.
While outside may be gloomy,
With no hope in near sight,
A flower will spring, souls trapped inside.
When valour dies in dead men's throats,
A poppy grows, safe is the soul inside.

While roses may be pretty,
And tulips dewy hills,
Under roots and weeds,
Springing from the grass,
Life through year and year,
The quiet flowers thrive.

While blossoms have a pretty face,
Covered in shining dew,
Hidden in the most obvious place,
Is where lay you,
Stereotyped as brainless,
Following herds and used for food,
Sheep are the hidden blossoms,
Not known for what they are.
When the darkness comes round,
Meaning is finally found,
Behind the neat rows of tulips and roses,
Behind the pretty face of pansy,
Lives the gentle daisy,
Only loved when the others disappear.

Teardrops

If the cold wind blows,
Will my teardrops still shine?
Will the stars whisper softly?
Will they be to far to reach?
Would the void in my belly bloom?
How will I be able to succumb?
Make this loneliness cease?

My teardrops will flow solemnly,
The stars will be too far to touch,
The void in my belly will grow and stretch,
And I won't be able to speak.
There will be no answer.
I will always be alone.
That's the way of my life,
That the way I disown.

If the world were a puzzle,
It would make a beautiful piece,
Colours and connections,
It would be lovely to see.
I would be part of that puzzle too,
But I wouldn't fit in.
Everyone would push me back.
And no matter how much I turned and twisted,

And shoved and cut,
I would always be alone.
Always be apart.

But that was until I found something,
An answer? A light?
A cloud gifted legs,
And impeccable sight.
He gave me confidence,
And helped me fit in.
The stars were getting brighter,
The wind was turning warm,
My teardrops were drying,
The answer was growing into more.

But a lamb cannot live forever,
And neither can his hope,
That bond was now breaking,
I'm my shell, all alone.
But his light in me still twinkles,
We will always be together,
But we will always be apart.

Gateway

In lush green fields,
Where the breeze carries freely,
And the birds fly far,
The gates are twinkling softly,
But, how to know what they are?
Inside this safe haven, happiness blooms,
But how to change, how to arise from anew?

Only when true danger is lived,
Can anything truly be safe.
Only when everything is nothing but space,
Can nothing touble you, or get in your way.

Inside this sacutaury, with nothing but light,
Nothing is safe, there is no reason to hide.
If the gateway stays open, can we jump right
through?
Experience the pains and joys to give us a clue?

The gateway is open,
Welcoming all,
While the world might be mean,
And heartless and cruel,
How can love be felt,
Without those feelings in too?

Even though the otherside is cold,
Filled with saddness and sorrow,
Glimers of gold will always shine through.
The medows will stay rich,
The breeze will carry hope,
The birds will sing with charity,
You will also stay the same,
But you will become different too,
Both in your mind and in your heart,
So from the ashes, out will walk you.

Time

While sometimes moments can strech forever,
And shrink to almost nothing,
While inside time can warp and move,
It always keeps its pace.
Some might think they can control time,
Make it stop or move,
But time is one of those invicible things,
And has to be lived full through.

Waiting for that moment,
When all would be changed,
For the better? For the worse?
For the in between?
Whatever it was, it had to be lived.
While it might be my monster,
While it might be my saviour,
It would haunt me forever.
The sun might shine,
The earth might go round,
The sorrow might invade,
But time sees no change.

The Distance

While he was far away,
Happy in his flock,
His adventure finally begun,
Slowing and stretching was the clock.

While this moment seemed cruel,
The heart turned cold,
The void had opened again,
Who knows when it would close?

While it seemed as if my life would break,
And my heart would never be whole,
And it felt as a open wound,
Rubbed and dusted with salt,
I knew that I would one day smile,
One day sing his song,
I could feel the void closing,
Gently, one by one.

That scar would be torn open,
Salt and vinigar now,
My heart had told the story, true,
My head had ingored wise wit.

While the distance that part us may be far,
He will ever remain in my heart,
His memory wil forever be ingrained in my
brain,
His song will forever rest in my soul.

Ancient Stars

The stars live far away,
Their home, the inky night,
The stars are our portals,
To the distant galaxies,
They show us the past,
Their lights, twinkling lines.
They turn the darkness of forever,
Into a glowing web of light.

They twinkle close enough to reach,
But stay to far away to touch.
Stars are the libraries,
They are stories, maps and gods,
Stars can sing gentle songs,
And guide us through the sea.
On painful nights,
When a wish is strong,
We turn our faces to them,
We whisper and wish for a better future,
And they hold that secret, safe.

Life was wished upon that lamb,
Yet it must have escaped their grip,
Maybe the stars are telling me,
That he was meant to die,
And that fate cannot be changed.

Forever stars have guided us,
And given us life and scope,
But they tell us when around is dark,
There is always that glint of hope.

Dead

He bounced through our life with joviality,
His spring that told it all,
His life was a public promise,
And death, a quiet lie.

People try to live forever,
As long as time allows,
But death is inevitable,
Though, for some it comes now.

He was only three months old,
A child finally gifted wings,
He seemed as if he would live forever,
But forthcoming was the dark.

A lie it seemed when we first found out,
An open, hidden void,
But, with every life comes an end,
And before every end, was a life.

Grief

Grief is a cloud that shifts and moves,
It's dark and grey and cold and sad,
It opens the void and sucks all in,
And triggers an unbearable nothing.

Sometimes emotions pelt you like rain,
Other times you feel an impeccable pain,
But more often you feel just nothing at all.
Lamb gave me soul and life,
Without him I was left a shell.
Sometimes that nothing hurt more than anything,
Sometimes it was just cold and taking.

I try to escape the claws of grief,
For a second I can smell fresh air,
And the breeze against my cheeks,
But grief is after me again,
And pulls me down to pain.

But grief does not last forever,
Just like lambs and hope,
From the dark of agony,
Arises new hope and integrity,
It offers a new set of eyes,
And a stronger, braver heart,

From the ashes of the grieving fire,
Walks acceptance,
And opportunity.

Healing Heart

Nothing is more beautiful,
Than a healing heart,
Stitches being sewn,
Cracks being nailed.
Love being found,
Trust being built.

Over time heart-ache can heal,
Growing stronger and braver,
A healed heart can be tougher,
Than the one before.
But healing heart is difficult,
And hurts and stings and kills,
But a healing heart,
Is one of those many things,
That can bring souls together,
And apart.
While a healing heart can be beautiful,
It can also be ugly,
While it can set prettily,
It can harden coldly.

Saying goodbye to a lamb,
Either "goodbye for now",
Or "goodbye forever",

Is a different type of crack,
One that insures loneliness,
And hurt and pain,
But it does not shatter it,
Nor does it chip,
It sends deep waves,
And fractures within.

But with every broken heart,
Comes a fixed opportunity,
While for a little time it hurts,
In the future it will be stronger,
And braver.
And kinder.
That healing heart will love more,
So the pain,
While it is deep and dreadful,
Is not completely in vain.

Opportunity

Opportunity has many forms,
And is not always set and solid,
It could be a path forged just for you,
Through trees and bushes,
It helps you find glory,
Whatever that might be.
Opportunity can go unseen for years,
A quiet hand pulling a shoulder,
It leads to to greatness,
And shows your true desire.

But opportunity can come,
When it is not expected at all,
In the darkness of the night,
Only to realise its dawn,
It can be simply a spark,
Deep inside your heart,
There is no clear path,
And no gentle guide,
Just an idea,
But no promise,
It could be dangerous,
It could be scary,
It could be worthy,
But it is opportunity.

Dark Depths

Even in the darkest depths,
Where no sun or warmth can reach,
Deep where nothing can be touched,
Can the peace finally teach.

The world is full of violence,
And mystery and control,
Torn apart by view and thoughts,
Yet still stitched together as a whole.

The human way of wanting,
Has taken so many lives,
Taken so many hopes,
And sparked too many lies.

Humans always want something,
Always must improve,
Must always take what must be ours,
Even though it can not move,
And can never be destroyed.
We live alongside nature,
And we work hand in hand,
So, why try and take that,
And change it to your plans?

What purpose do the wars have?
To what purpose is the want?
To what purpose is the laziness,
And growing need for gaunt,
To what purpose is the killing,
And making lives so hard,
We only have one to live,
So why send all the disregard?

Nature wants us to work in harmony,
To live among the plants,
To work and grow and give and more,
But that opportunity has depart.

All the wars and protests
Are now just the past,
Why change what cannot be changed?
Why not all come together and use what is last?

But the inner piece of beauty,
Seen by the blind eye,
Is what connects all humans,
No matter race comply,
A safe haven we go to lay,
Where nothing can defy.

We are all just puppets,
Playing natures games.
In that place not cursed by light,

In that place where all is calm,
Can true life and light be uncovered,
And love, finally restored.

Little Things

Stepping into the forest,
With no promise for the future,
Following unused trails,
Singing unheard songs,
Taking every sidetrack,
Using every challenge.
Climbing every hill,
Swimming every lake,
That's living life,
Completed and whole.

You may face ditches,
You may face thorns,
You may face pitfalls,
You may be alone,
But finding love and chasing it,
Is worth all that chance,
For when love is truly felt,
No challenge is too great.
For while life might be tough,
It is beautiful too,
It's full of love and kindness,
It's full of fun and change,
It's full of the little moments,
That make someone's day.

Its when you hold the door for someone,
Or tie their shoe,
Stop to sniff the roses,
Or saying "I love you",
Life is full of little things,
That make it so sweet,
Life is too short,
So only little things remain.

No one needs the drama,
The giant speech and acts,
The little nudges and ideas,
Is all that is needed,
To show care and love,
And the in between.
The little acts of kindness,
Colour in the picture.

Life is so beautiful,
If only we could see,
Beyond the acts and wishes,
Behind the pretty tulips,
The shy smiles that light up your eyes,
And gentle hugs that are still too tight,
And quiet laughs that have love inside.
The little bugs,
The tiny bees,
When put together,
Sadness leaves.

Story

Stories, long and dark,
Can tell of light and valour,
But, there is an end.